[UNDERSTANDING GRAMMAR]

COMMON GRAMMATICAL MISTAKES

ANN RIGGS

CREATIVE ☾ EDUCATION

Published by Creative Education
P.O. Box 227, Mankato, Minnesota 56002
Creative Education is an imprint of The Creative Company
www.thecreativecompany.us

Design and production by Liddy Walseth
Art direction by Rita Marshall
Printed by Corporate Graphics in the United States of America

Photographs by Getty Images (Thomas Barwick, Alistair Berg, Burazin, Christian Kober,
Cyril Laubscher, MoMo Productions, Steve Morenos/Newspix, Magnus Ragnvid, Andy Ryan, Joel Sartore,
Kim Taylor, Art Wolfe), iStockphoto (Jill Battaglia, by_nicholas, Michael Cogliantry, Matthew Dixon,
FotoVoyager, Lisa Gagne, Eric Isselée, Valerii Kaliuzhnyi, Natasha Litova, Narvikk, Sadeugra,
Natalia Sinjushina, Ramona Smiers, Prapass Wahnapinij)

Library of Congress Cataloging-in-Publication Data
Riggs, Ann.
Common grammatical mistakes / by Ann Riggs.
p. cm. — (Understanding grammar)
Includes bibliographical references and index.
Summary: An examination of the rules behind English grammar, focusing on the most common mistakes made
by writers—including dangling participles, run-on sentences, and misused words—and how to fix them.
ISBN 978-1-60818-092-9
1. English language—Errors of usage. 2. English language—Grammar. I. Title. II. Series.
PE1460.R523 2010
428—dc22   2010028300

CPSIA: 110310PO1386

First Edition
2 4 6 8 9 7 5 3 1

TABLE of CONTENTS

Music swells. Siblings squabble. Owls hoot. I am. Grammar is.

And just like that, two words can become a SENTENCE. The information in a short sentence can be expanded by adding more words that give vivid descriptions or specific reactions. Where should those words be placed? How does a writer know what PUNCTUATION to use? What does all of that mean, anyway? Words fall into place more easily when one has an understanding of grammar, a system of rules that gives writers the foundation for producing acceptable, formal expression. It is that acceptable form, that appropriate grammar, which helps readers comprehend what has been written.

The whole point of understanding grammar is to gain the knowledge of how to write correctly and then apply it to your work. Writers write; readers read. Believe it or not, correct usage may keep writers from making embarrassing mistakes. Learning the lessons of acceptable usage will not only improve your writing, but it will also lead you to a better understanding of the structure behind it, a system known as STANDARD WRITTEN ENGLISH (SWE).

SWE has been agreed upon by most publishers, colleges, and standardized test developers to be the most correct and the most understandable form of written English. No matter what part of North America one may call home, we all can take comfort in having a common system of written grammar and expression, thanks to SWE. Regardless of how a person's speech sounds, despite regional or social differences in dialect, the rules are the same. While dialect makes a native of Boston, Massachusetts's speech sound different from that of a native of Dallas, Texas, their formal written English should look the same.

Grammar provides the backbone of language, and learning it is a significant part of acquiring any language, from French and Spanish to Mandarin and Hindi. Because correct expression is fundamental to communication, classes in grammar and composition have been taught since the Middle Ages. That means that for the past 500 to 1,500 years, teachers have been trying to impress upon their students the importance of correct, grammatical expression.

HANGING ON
FOR DEAR LIFE

Despite our teachers' best efforts, some of us still get confused about grammar when we try to move from lists of rules to actual writing. We may understand that adjectives MODIFY nouns and pronouns; we can write examples that answer *which?*, *how many?*, and *what kind?* of people, places, and things. We can put these words into phrases and clauses and recognize them, even when they look like verbs. Then we try to write sentences, and sometimes we end up with an unfortunate result such as this:

Flitting from flower to flower,

the football player watched the bee.

The MAIN CLAUSE has a subject (*football player*) and a verb (*watched*); that's fine. "Flitting from flower to flower" is an *-ing* adjective phrase and is supposed to be describing a noun or pronoun—which leads us to *football player*? That's a problem. This common mistake is called a dangling participle because "flitting" is a participle, a word formed from a verb that acts as an adjective, and it has been left hanging with no logical noun or pronoun to modify. We need to make some changes. The football player clearly is not flitting from flower to flower, so what is?

Flitting from flower to flower, the bee caught the football player's attention.

Changing the wording solves our dilemma; the bee can flit from flower to flower. The PARTICIPIAL PHRASE that begins the sentence is supposed to modify what immediately follows; readers expect it to work that way, even if they don't know exactly what a participial phrase is. If that isn't the way the sentence is constructed, the participle, as well as the reader, is left dangling. Let's try another. If we want to write about a lioness and her cubs, we may write:

The lion cubs were protected from danger. The lioness was watching constantly.

But when we want all the information in one sentence, we need to be careful to not write this:

Watching constantly, the lion cubs were protected from danger.

What watched them? The cubs themselves? That's not what we meant to say. We know what we meant—that the lioness was on the scene—but when we wrote about it, we were thinking about the cubs. That's a clue to identifying

and correcting a dangling participle—subject placement. The adjective phrase "watching constantly" needs to be placed next to the noun it really modifies, "lioness."

Watching constantly, the lioness protected her cubs from danger.

That's much better. As another example, consider this word picture:

Jack watched his horse take a turn around the racetrack carrying a lap time sheet under his arm.

There's a horse that really wants to keep track of his time! Or perhaps not. Restating this sentence by putting the phrase at the beginning of the sentence clarifies both the participle and its subject:

Carrying a lap time sheet under his arm, Jack watched his horse take a turn around the racetrack.

We've found an acceptable solution. Sometimes a PREPOSITIONAL PHRASE is the culprit when it comes to dangling participles. Seeing a phrase that begins with a preposition such as *at*, *by*, *to*, *for*, or *on* should cause a reader to proceed with caution; there may be a dangerous dangling participle ahead. For example, how would you interpret the following sentence?

At the age of nine, my mom persuaded my dad to buy me a puppy.

DANGLING PARTICIPLE

As the sentence currently reads, your mother was very young when you were born. This, unfortunately, has created a new problem: a misplaced modifier. What that means is that the noun or pronoun being modified is in the wrong part of the sentence or, as is the case with our example, it is missing entirely. What is the effect? The reader attaches the adjective phrase "at the age of nine" to the wrong noun, "mom." Ask yourself, "Who is nine?" Then put that information near the prepositional phrase.

When I was nine years old, my mom persuaded my dad to buy me a puppy.

Inserting "I" and "was" gives the nine-year-old the correct explanation. Misplaced modifiers are tricky. If we're not careful, the dangling participle or misplaced modifier can entirely change what we mean to say. Instead of **After falling from the tree, my uncle picked up the apple**, try **After the apple fell from the tree, my uncle picked it up.** Now the sentence's meaning is clear. Do you see why learning about danglers and misplaced parts is so important?

Mastering this concept as a younger writer can save you years of frustration and rewriting. After all, business professionals are expected to be able to communicate effectively as part of their jobs. In 1992, American businessman Tom Sant wrote *Persuasive Business Proposals: Writing to Win Customers, Clients, and Contracts*. It sold so well that he revised the book and reissued it in 2004. Can you guess what one of the errors is that Sant mentions in his discussion about how to write business proposals? Yes, indeed—the dangling participle. Here's an example from the book:

After rotting in the cellar for weeks, my brother brought up some oranges.

Wow! Your decomposing brother is trying to be helpful? Think again. How can we make certain the rotten oranges are dealt with and assure your brother that he doesn't have to stay in the basement?

My brother brought up some oranges that had been rotting in the cellar for weeks.

There. No dangling or misplacement; no questionable treatment of family members. Students of good writing do have choices. They can either learn to use correct grammar while they're in school, or they can waste their bosses' time by being retrained on the job as adults. Even if their employment isn't in a company that requires them to write persuasive proposals, employees may find that they need to write e-mails, letters, articles, or evaluations. All of these occasions are opportunities to communicate in writing. While the administrative assistants are on vacation, some volunteers may be faced with revising information such as this:

HANG ON

The concert held in Fellowship Hall was a great success. Special

thanks are due to the minister's daughter, who labored the whole evening at the piano, which as usual fell upon her.

The dangling idea of "falling" is too far away from "daughter," the noun it modifies, and is too near the wrong noun, "piano." The piano didn't fall on anyone; the responsibility of accompanying, or playing the piano, did. Let's fix it: **Special thanks go to the minister's daughter, who provided the piano accompaniment the whole evening.** Our problem is solved. Whenever you encounter dangling modifiers or participles, hang on to your common sense and reword until you can match the correct noun with its modifier.

Having Second Thoughts

Modifiers that are not next to the words they describe often cause misinterpretations. Rewrite the following sentences, making sure participles aren't dangling and modifiers aren't far removed. You may have to add words of your own to fix the problems.

THE DOCTOR TOLD THE PATIENT TO TAKE THE MEDICINE TWICE EVERY DAY, STANDING IN THE DOORWAY.

WHEN MULTIPLYING BY 5's THE NUMBERS ALWAYS END IN 5 OR 0.

HAVING EATEN THE REMAINS OF THE ZEBRA, WE WATCHED THE LION LICK HIS CHOPS.

DASHING MADLY FOR THE BUS, DWIGHT'S PAPERS FELL OUT OF HIS ARMS.

WHEN ONLY A SMALL BOY, MY FATHER TOOK ME WITH HIM TO CHICAGO.

ALWAYS THREATENING RAIN, WE GLARED AT THE DARK SKY.

TOO LITTLE, TOO MUCH, OR JUST RIGHT

In their book *Sleeping Dogs Don't Lay: Practical Advice for the Grammatically Challenged* (1999), Richard Lederer (1938–) and Richard Dowis (1930–) make this point: "[U]sing bad grammar can mark a person as one who is careless of language and who may be, by extension, careless of other things. Most of us, most of the time, need to respect the rules and conventions of grammar." The rules Lederer and Dowis talk about dictate that sentences must have a subject and a verb that form a complete thought. When writers get in a hurry—get careless—they sometimes discover one of two things is wrong with their sentences: either not enough information is there or too many thoughts have been fused together.

First, let's deal with the shortchanged word groups. A group of words that begins with a capital letter and ends with a period is not automatically a sentence. Without an INDEPENDENT CLAUSE that has a subject and a verb, there is no complete thought; all incomplete thoughts are called fragments. Here's an example of a fragment: **In California during the recent wildfires and after the torrential rains that followed.** Three prepositional phrases don't make up for the lack of a subject and a verb. Both need to be added: **In California, during the recent wildfires and after the torrential rains that followed, many *people* lost their homes.** The subject, "people," and the verb phrase, "lost their homes," were just what the fragment needed to become a complete thought —and thus a complete sentence.

Other fragments may begin with participles, such as **Working far into the night, attempting to harvest the corn crop.** There is action, but not as a main verb, and who is doing the harvesting? The incomplete thought needs both verb and subject to be supplied: **Working far into the night, attempting to harvest the corn crop, area *farmers tried* to beat the rain that was forecast.** Adding "farmers" as the subject and "tried" as the verb saves the

sentence. Now what if the subject is there, but no verb appears? ***Some* of the vacationers at the beach last summer.** That word group just leaves us hanging, even though we know the subject, "some." With the addition of a verb phrase, it becomes a complete sentence: **Some of the vacationers at the beach last summer *discovered* just how effective sunscreen can be.**

Fragments may also be victims of dependent clauses, groups of words that already have a subject and a verb but don't make an independent thought: **Since she had done the math assignments and reviewed**

for the test. Then what happened? We have a COMPOUND VERB (*had done/reviewed*) and a subject (*she*), but the words are tied up in a SUBORDINATE CLAUSE that needs the help of an absent main clause. We can fix that by adding a subject and a verb that can stand alone: **Since she had done the math assignments and reviewed for the test, *Roxie felt confident.*** What is the main clause? "Roxie felt confident." That independent word group supports the dependent clause before it. The sentence is now complete.

What about sentences that contain too much information? This problem doesn't have anything to do with the number of words used. After all, our sentence about Roxie is as complete a thought with 3 words as it is with 15. What we're talking about is having too many independent clauses, parts that can really be on their own but are punctuated as if they were one complete thought. This is known as a run-on sentence—just because one capital letter begins it and one punctuation mark ends it, that doesn't mean it's correct. Short sentences can be run-ons just as easily as longer ones can: **The sun was hot Jan nearly fainted.** Can you find the two separate clauses? (1) "The sun was hot." (2) "Jan nearly fainted." Actually, that is one solution to a run-on—make two (or more) short sentences out of it. But the question we should ask is whether the parts are related enough to be in the same sentence. For this pair, the answer is

THE SUN WAS HOT

yes; they have a cause-and-effect connection. (The cause is the hot sun, and the effect is that Jan nearly fainted.) Therefore, we have choices in remedying the problem. One solution is to separate the independent clauses with a comma and a coordinating conjunction (*and, but, for, or, nor, so, yet*): **The sun was hot, and Jan nearly fainted.** Another solution is to divide them equally with a semicolon (;): **The sun was hot; Jan nearly fainted.**

We've succeeded in stopping the run-on by adding punctuation and, in one case, a connecting word, *and*. These are standard options for solving run-on dilemmas, no matter how many words are in the sentence. The main thing is to be sure to split the independent

parts with the accepted punctuation and conjunction. Examine this, for instance: **The sun was hot, Jan nearly fainted.** Do you see what happened? There is punctuation, and it's in the right place, but a comma isn't strong enough to hold the main clauses apart. This error is known as a comma splice. It's the wrong way to connect independent clauses—it uses a comma but no conjunction and is an error to avoid in writing good COMPOUND and COMPOUND-COMPLEX SENTENCES. When words such as *and* and *or* tie stand-alone sentence parts together, place a comma before the conjunction. Using the comma by itself may seem to be a way of joining clauses, and you

may think it looks good or that you need to pause there, and perhaps you do, but using only the comma is not correct. Look at the structure of the previous sentence. The comma + conjunction construction was used three times! Look at the following example with fewer words: **The wind was cold, the girls decided not to walk.** That was merely spliced together. Correctly put together, the sentence will use both a comma and a conjunction: **The wind was cold, so the girls decided not to walk.**

Piecing sentence parts together with only a comma can be a problem for run-ons of any length. Take a look at the following example:

Mrs. Johnson told us that the next chapter of the novel has information in it that is difficult to understand, I'll need to spend all weekend reading my book and not watch any of my regular TV shows.

We can make two separate sentences, removing the comma and putting a period after the first "understand." Or we can replace the comma with a semicolon.

Mrs. Johnson told us that the next chapter of the novel has information in it that is difficult to understand; I'll need to spend all weekend reading my book and not watch any of my regular TV shows.

Another option is to keep the comma and add the conjunction *so*. One more choice is to use a transitional expression such as a CONJUNCTIVE ADVERB appropriate to the meaning. A semicolon is used to close the first clause, and a word such as *however* or *therefore*, followed by a comma, signals the beginning of the second clause:

Mrs. Johnson told us that the next chapter of the novel has information in it that is difficult to understand; therefore, I'll need to spend all weekend reading my book and not watch any of my regular TV shows.

The best solution is not to write run-ons in the first place or to catch them when proofreading—carefully reading your work before submitting it and then making corrections. This is also what good writers do.

BUILD YOUR OWN SENTENCE
Picking Up the Pieces

A sentence fragment is a group of words that isn't a complete thought and can't exist by itself in formal writing. Your job is to fix the broken sentence parts that follow. Add a subject and a verb and write a complete sentence for each of the fragments on the opposite page. Don't let the capital letters and end punctuation fool you—none of these is a whole sentence.

1. FOOTBALL GAME ON SATURDAY.
2. WHICH ALWAYS THROWS A MONKEY WRENCH INTO DAD'S PLANS.
3. AFFECTED BY YEARS OF NEGLECT.
4. WHILE WE STOOD IN LINE FOR HOURS!
5. UNLESS YOU COUNT TWO PET GERBILS NAMED SPIN AND MARTY.
6. ONE SCOOP OF MINT CHOCOLATE CHIP AND ONE OF SUPER FUDGE BROWNIE.

ONLY IF YOU MEAN IT

Entire sentences cannot be blamed for all the grammatical mistakes we encounter; sometimes it's the smallest words or phrases that are the biggest troublemakers. Let's examine some that are often misused and misunderstood: *as*, *as if*, *like*, and *such as*. The first two are conjunctions; the other two are prepositions. Let's look more closely at the difference. When the word *as* is used, look for the subject and verb that follow it; *as* begins a dependent clause and links it to a main clause: **As he grew older, he kept more to himself.** The words after *as*, the subject "he" and the verb "grew," are part of the dependent clause. That means *as* is a conjunction. Some-times *as* is used with *if*. *As if* and *as though* mean "as would be the case if." For instance, **Jeb was told to dress *as if* he were meeting his grandfather for the first time.** Words following *as* and *if* show their connections to clauses: *as if* begins the dependent clause that contains the subject "he" and the verb "were meeting." That dependent clause is joined to the main clause of the sentence with its subject "Jeb" and verb "was told." All of those words work together well.

When the misused word *like* is substituted for *as if*, it brings trouble: **Jeb was told to dress *like* he were meeting his grandfather for the first time.** By definition, *like*

isn't a conjunction that precedes a subject and verb; it's a preposition that needs to be followed by a noun or pronoun in the OBJECTIVE CASE. In the "dressing" sentence, the word after *like* is the subject pronoun, "he"; it's not an object (a person or thing that a preposition relates to another word or word group). *Like* isn't a connecting word and should not be used that way in formal expression. Keep in mind that our goal is to learn the standard English form. In sentences explaining comparisons, the conjunction construction *as ... as* is used: **She's as tall as her mother; she's not as tall as her father, though.** Why do we use *as*? The sentence is an example of an incomplete comparison and really means "as tall as her mother *is*." The verb isn't visible but is implied. It may seem confusing, but that's the reason *as ... as* is preferred to **She's tall like her mother.** What that sentence really means is "She's tall like her mother *is*." When we see the subject, "mother," and the verb, "is"—whether shown or merely implied—we recognize the word group as a clause that needs the conjunction *as*, not the preposition *like*.

When is it appropriate to use *like*? It's correctly used in these sentences: **Colby has never been to a school *like* ours, What's he *like*?,** and **I've never met anyone *like* him.** In each of these cases, *like* is a preposition preceding an object: "*like* ours." "*like* What?" and "*like* him." The word *like* means "similar to" and refers to a category of things that closely resemble each other. In our examples, the categories were one school versus all schools and one person versus other people. In contrast, the phrase *such as* refers to specific things, rather than those in a broad category: **Wild elephants spend most of their time looking for and eating foods *such as* grass, leaves, flowers, fruits, and twigs.** Since the foods are not all the same, *such as* is a better choice than *like* is.

It may seem as if we're being too particular about grammatical preferences, but readers do judge writers by their words. If what a writer says is substandard, incorrect grammar, the reader's first impression will be a poor one, making the writer appear uneducated. One of the worst impressions is given when two negatives are used in one sentence. Double negatives are deadly! The words hardly, barely, and *scarcely* are negative in effect, as is *n't*, the CONTRACTION of *not*. Using such words in any combination makes more than one negative statement in a sentence. In standard English expression, two negatives do not make a positive, and three are even worse. Here are some

samples of what to avoid and what to substitute.

(1) **I didn't do nothing! I didn't say nothing to her!** The *n't* and the word *nothing* are both negative. Instead say, **I didn't do anything! I didn't say anything to her!** In other words, you didn't talk back.

(2) **Hardly nobody stayed for the meeting.** The two negative words *hardly* and *nobody* make the double negative. Correct it by saying, **Hardly anybody stayed for the meeting.** What you mean is that few people attended, right?

(3) **The poor child isn't scarcely wearing nothing at all.** This sentence has three negative words: *isn't*, *scarcely*, and *nothing*. What you want to say is, **The poor child is scarcely wearing anything at all.** When you're concerned about a child needing more clothing, one negative reference carries the message.

Remember, we're concerned with English communication and standards. It is true that there are some foreign languages that view double negatives as correct, but your readers—and your teachers—of English are not going to excuse such language errors, so be careful to avoid them.

Cutting It in Half

Using double negatives means including more than one negative element in a sentence. Resolve the following negative troubles by choosing only one of the elements (*no*, *not*, *n't*, *neither*, *never*, *nothing*, *nobody*, *hardly*, *scarcely*) in each sentence and rewriting the statements. Hint: "nothing" may become "anything," and "no" may become "any."

1. HE DIDN'T HAVE NO LUNCH.

2. SHE CAN'T HARDLY STAND IT.

3. THEY NEVER SAID NOTHING TO NOBODY.

4. WENDELL COULDN'T SEE HIM NEITHER.

5. THERE WEREN'T NO PIES LIKE GRANDMA'S.

6. THERE WASN'T SCARCELY ENOUGH MONEY.

7. THE PILOT COULD NOT FIND NOWHERE TO LAND.

8. ARIZONA HAD HARDLY NO RAIN LAST SUMMER.

ANSWER KEY

1. He didn't have any lunch. Or: He had no lunch. 2. She can hardly stand it. 3. They never said anything to anybody. 4. Wendell couldn't see him, either. 5. There were no pies like Grandma's. Or: There weren't any pies like Grandma's. 6. There was scarcely enough money. 7. The pilot could find nowhere to land. Or: The pilot could not find anywhere to land. 8. Arizona had hardly any rain last summer.

THE CASE IN QUESTION

Another category of mistakes also involves word choices that are often confusing. *Who*, *which*, and *that* are relative pronouns, meaning they each can be the first word of a dependent clause and relate it to the main part of the sentence. *Who* is the only one of the three that changes form—becomes another word—when it changes its case, or its use in the sentence. When it is in the NOMINATIVE CASE, *who* can be the subject or a PREDICATE nominative, renaming the subject from the verb side of the sentence. In short, *who* does something.

The sentence **Strickland Gillilan was the poet who wrote "I Had a Mother Who Read to Me"** shows that the main clause (*Strickland Gillilan was the poet*) and the dependent clause (*who wrote 'I Had a Mother Who Read to Me'*) are related. *Who* is the subject of the subordinate clause that tells more about the author. Isolating that clause gives us a way to see what it would be like with the pronoun *he* instead of *who*. Saying "*he* wrote the poem" proves we need a nominative case pronoun for the subject; that means we need *who*. What's also interesting about this sentence is the title of that poem and its use of the relative pronoun. *Who* is correct in the title for the same reasons that it's correct in the sentence itself; the dependent clause (*who read to* *me*) can be thought of as "she read to me," and the nominative case matches the subject (*who*) twice in one sentence.

The objective case form of *who* is *whom*. It can be a DIRECT OBJECT; an indirect object; or an object of a preposition, an infinitive (formed with "to" and a verb, used as a noun), or a gerund (an -*ing* verb used as a noun). That means *whom* has something done to it; it's never the doer. Take a look at the following sentence: **A benefactor *whom* the administrator declined to name paid off the balance of the mortgage.** Let's find the main clause first, so we don't confuse it with the subordinate one: "A benefactor paid off the balance of the mortgage." That leaves the clause "*whom* the administrator declined to name," which already has a subject, "administrator," and a verb, "declined." The relative pronoun *whom* is the object of the infinitive "to name" and needs to be in the objective case. Is that confusing? Try substituting the objective case pronoun *him*

for *whom* to check it out: "The administrator declined to name *him*." The objective case fits, because the nominative case *he* doesn't: "The administrator declined to name *he*." Nope. Even if we don't know that *whom* is the object of the infinitive, when *him* is correct, *whom* is, too. Besides, we picked out "administrator" as the subject of the clause, so that job was taken. We have no use for "who" as a subject. *Whom* therefore wins.

A good rule of thumb when trying to decide between using *who* or *whom* is to replace the word with a pronoun such as *she/her* or *he/him* and figure out if you need the nominative or the objective case. Here's a more common example: **The letter began: "To Whom It May Concern."** In that letter salutation, *whom* is the object of the preposition *to*. Using our

substitution, we know to say "to *him*" not "to *he*," using the objective case *him*, rather than the nominative, *he*. That verifies our choice of *whom*.

Now to the question of ownership. When you want *who* to show ownership, or possession, use *whose*, the POSSESSIVE form of the pronoun, as in **The skier *whose* time was the fastest won the medal.** Since the person who won had the fastest time, *whose* gives possession to that skier. We can remove the main clause, "The skier won the medal," to get a closer look at the dependent part in question: "*whose* time was the fastest." Substituting the possessive pronoun *his* for *whose* would read, "*his* time was the fastest," and this shows our possessive choice, *whose*, is the correct one. All three— *who*, *whom*, and *whose*—are used only when a

pronoun is referring to a person.

Which refers to an animal or a thing but not a person, and it is usually set off by a comma. A *which* clause adds information, but it doesn't change the meaning of the main clause. Take a look at the following: **Vancouver, British Columbia, *which* was selected in 2003, was the site for the 2010 Winter Olympic Games.** The *which* clause isn't restricted to the sentence—we can take it out of the sentence without affecting the meaning: **Vancouver, British Columbia, was the site for the 2010 Winter Olympic Games.**

The relative pronoun *that* is the most versatile; it can refer to a person, animal, or a thing. *That* is used to narrow a category or identify a particular item of a larger class, such as **Any vehicle *that* is taller than 10 feet (3 m) will not fit into the car wash bay.** The *that* clause contains information necessary to the sentence. It restricts it to a particular classification—in this case, the height of a vehicle. The pronoun *that* can be used wherever *who* or *which* can, so if you want to play it safely—and if you're too confused to pick one—use *that*.

Adding *-ever* to *who*, *whom*, and *which* forms the compound words *whoever*, *whomever*, and *whichever*, and these words follow the same rules as their simpler counterparts. For instance, in the sentence **We should ask *whoever* is responsible for the refreshments to tell us why there isn't enough cake,** using *whoever* is correct as the subject of the clause and its verb, "is" (*whoever is responsible*). However, the entire clause also has a use in the sentence, and this time it serves as

the direct object of the action "should ask." Remember to isolate the *whoever* clause first to avoid being confused by its use in the sentence. Otherwise it may look as though we should ask *whomever*, just because we do need a direct object for the main clause. Check by substituting a subject pronoun, such as *she*: "*She* is responsible for the refreshments." If we try the objective case, thinking we're substituting for *whomever*, we use *her*. But, no, we don't want to be stuck with "*Her* is responsible for the refreshments." *She* is the subject; *whoever* is the subject form. That's why it is correct. Before we leave this ho-humming of who-whom-ing, keep this in mind: It's not *who* you know; it's *whom* you know that really counts. Beyond that, it's knowing the rules of grammar that gives you an edge.

IT'S NOT WHO YOU KNOW; IT'S WHOM YOU KNOW

Pointing in the Right Direction

Below are three sentences that properly use *who* and *whom*. Your job is to figure out why each is correct. First, write each sentence as it is. Then write only the independent clause. Next, name the subject, verb, and object or predicate nominative in the dependent clause. We know *who* can be used as a subject or predicate nominative, and *whom* can be used as an object. Now it's your turn to justify these sentences:

1. THE GIRL WHO WINS THE RACE WILL ADVANCE TO THE SEMIFINALS.
2. DO YOU KNOW WHO IT MIGHT BE?
3. COLLEEN IS A GIRL WHOM WE ALL KNOW AND TRUST.

ANSWER KEY

1. Independent clause: The girl will advance to the semifinals
Dependent clause: who (subject) wins (verb) race (direct object)
2. Independent clause: you do know
Dependent clause: it (subject) might be (linking verb) who (predicate nominative)
3. Independent clause: Colleen is a girl
Dependent clause: we (subject) know/trust (verb) whom (direct object)

MAKING WISE CHOICES

hat we've covered so far is an argument for using correct expression because of its importance to you and I, right? Well, yes and no. Using correct expression is important, but saying it incorrectly ruins everything. What is wrong with the first sentence in this paragraph? Think about grammar and its importance *to us*. "To us" is a prepositional phrase; prepositions need to be followed by the objective case. *You* isn't the pronoun in question; that same word is used for both nominative and objective cases. The problem is *I*. The prepositional phrase "to you and me" correctly states our case. Are compounds confusing? Perhaps the problem is the conjunction *and*. Take it out. If deciding between saying, **The waitress gave Rudolph and *I* our food** and **The waitress gave Rudolph and *me* our food**, be selfish and deal only with the choice of *I* or *me*. That leaves this: "The waitress gave *I* my food" or "The waitress gave *me* my food." It's dangerous to make choices based on what sounds correct, but in this case, even if we don't know the sen-

tence requires an objective case pronoun as the direct object of "gave," saying "she gave *I* my food" just isn't right. That means the sentence should be written this way: **The waitress gave Rudolph and *me* our food.** Use that logic in deciding about compound subjects, too. For instance, ***She* and *I* think alike** is correct; ***Her* and *I* think alike** isn't. How can we tell? Split the pronouns: "*She* thinks" or "*Her* thinks"? *She* really does.

Similar problems arise with verbs. A basic rule (with some exceptions) is that verbs with -*s* are singular, and verbs without -*s* are plural. That sounds contrary to what we know about singular versus plural nouns, but it is true for many verbs. Apply the -*s* rule to the following: **We *was* surprised to see you there last night.** The verb *was* ends in -*s*; it is to be used with singular nouns and pronouns: "he was," "I was," "it was." Therefore, the sentence with a plural subject should read, **We *were* surprised.** The ending -*s* idea works for action verbs, too: "she writes," but "they write." Other verb dilemmas involve misusing helping verbs. *Has* ends in -*s*. Use it with a singular subject, and also include it with the past participle—don't leave it off. Say this: **She *has seen* that movie 16 times!** Avoid even thinking of saying this: **She *seen* that movie.** The same is true for choosing to say *does* or *do* and whether to add a helper with *did* or *done*. Here are correct examples: **Julie *does* so well on her own. She *did* her homework all by herself.** The following is not correct: **Julie *done* her homework.** Neither is this: **All the boys *done* their pushups.** No, they *didn't*.

Writing improves with practice and exposure to other good writing. You may *suppose* that good writers are *supposed* to know the characteristics of acceptable grammar; they're

used (not *use*) to relying on the rules of formal expression. Maybe we could say we have to "use it or *lose* it" when it comes to applying word choices. What we do know for sure is that we can't let *loose* ends trip us up. Never think that what you're writing has no *effect* on others; you *affect* them every time you present a well-written opinion, *regardless* (never *ir*regardless) of others' views. But your readers, when *they're* given opportunities to ponder *their* viewpoints, may find *you're* able to change their thinking. *Your* ability to communicate may not seem *too* important *to* you now, but it will *later*. Of the *two* choices, giving up on trying to understand grammar or making it a priority, the *latter* should be your goal.

We can hope that people will give us the benefit of the doubt, in spite of our grammatical errors. But our mistakes have consequences. If our readers see grammatical errors, they may think we don't know what we're talking about, even if we are experts, and our credibility is shot. Good writers must be alert and choose words that fit the rules. "It doesn't sound right" isn't an authentic guide unless a person has heard words used correctly. Teachers of English as a second language challenge English speakers to improve our speaking. Hearing ourselves speak the right words helps us write them correctly. That can be a challenge, because many people don't know what they don't know. In the meantime, grammar gives us guidelines. No one will be distracted by our errors if we don't make any.

Paul Brians, (1942–) a former English professor at Washington State University in Pullman, Washington, offers this analysis in his 2003 book, *Common Errors in English Usage*:

" No list of errors—no matter how diligently memorized—can make you into a fine writer. Nothing beats lots of reading and writing. But the sad truth is that few students read or write much these days, and most of it is done in the ANARCHIC setting of e-mail and chat rooms, where 'correctness' is scorned. It is not uncommon for students to make it all the way through school without having their writing thoroughly scrutinized and critiqued until they encounter disaster in the form of a picky professor, editor, or boss. Many businesses consider standard English usage a prime requirement for employment in responsible positions. "

STANDARD PORTABLE TYPEWRITER

Where can we get a crash course in correctness? Nowhere in particular. Good writers study. Good writers write. Good writers ask for help, seeing if others' impressions of what has been written are the same as theirs. We often use a dictionary to check our word choices, but we must remember what that source really is: a dictionary is an alphabetical collection of words used in our language. After all, *ain't* is in the dictionary, but that doesn't mean it is acceptable in standard English. "I am not" has no contraction. But that's no reason to write "I ain't going." Saying that leads nowhere, and it's imperative that careful writers go somewhere else, leading their readers with them.

GOOD WRITERS READ

BUILD YOUR OWN SENTENCE
Knowing the Difference

Does this sentence sound right to you? "It was our job to see that the doors were locked; the responsibility fell to him and me." Look closely at the last four words: "to him and me." From whatever source you need, find out why those words are the correct choice. Write your explanation in a complete sentence, telling the name of the expression (the kind of phrase) and what case the pronouns *him* and *me* are. Now make more wise choices by writing separate sentences to show your understanding of the definition of each of these often-confused words: *their/they're*; *later/latter*; *suppose/supposed*, and *your/you're*.

ANSWER KEY

The prepositional phrase, "to him and me," requires objective case pronouns, "him" and "me."

GLOSSARY

anarchic: without rules or order

compound sentences: sentences that have two or more independent clauses that are often joined by a comma and a conjunction

compound verb: two or more verbs used with the same subject in one clause or sentence

compound-complex sentences: sentences composed of elements of both a compound sentence and a complex sentence (two or more independent clauses and at least one dependent clause)

conjunctive adverb: a word or transitional expression that connects clauses in a sentence and functions as an adverb modifier, describing how, when, where, how much, or why about a verb, an adjective, or another adverb

contraction: a shortened form of a word or group of words, with the missing letters usually marked by an apostrophe

direct object: the person or thing that receives the action of a transitive verb

independent clause: two or more words with a subject and a verb that make one complete thought

main clause: a group of words with a subject and a verb that makes sense by itself and to which other dependent clauses may be connected

modify: to describe, limit, or qualify a word

nominative case: the classification of nouns and pronouns that function as subjects and predicate nominatives (*I, we, you, he, she, it, they*)

objective case: the classification of nouns and pronouns that function as receivers of action or as objects of prepositions (*me, us, you, him, her, it, them*)

participial phrase: two or more words that begin with a verb ending in *-ing* or *-ed* (or an irregular form) that function as an adjective in modifying a noun or pronoun

possessive: showing ownership of something; the classification of nouns and pronouns that show possession

predicate: the part of a clause or sentence containing a verb and stating something about the subject

prepositional phrase: a group of words consisting of a preposition (*at, by, of, to,* etc.), its object, and any modifiers

punctuation: marks used to provide meaning and separate elements within sentences, such as periods, commas, question marks, exclamation points, semicolons, colons, hyphens, and parentheses

sentence: a unit of expression that contains a subject and a verb and expresses a complete, independent thought

Standard Written English: the generally accepted model for educated English speech and writing that has no regional variations

subordinate clause: a group of words with a subject and verb that cannot stand alone; also known as a dependent clause

SELECTED BIBLIOGRAPHY

Brians, Paul. *Common Errors in English Usage*. Wilsonville, Ore.: William, James & Co., 2003.

The Chicago Manual of Style. 15th ed. Chicago: The University of Chicago Press, 2003.

Darling, Charles. "Guide to Grammar." Capital Community College Foundation. http://grammar.ccc.commnet.edu/grammar/.

Hodges, John C., Winifred B. Horner, Suzanne S. Webb, and Robert K. Miller. *Harbrace College Handbook*. 13th ed. Fort Worth, Tex.: Harcourt Brace College Publishers, 1998.

Lederer, Richard, and Richard Dowis. *Sleeping Dogs Don't Lay: Practical Advice for the Grammatically Challenged*. New York: St. Martin's Press, 1999.

O'Conner, Patricia T. *Woe Is I: The Grammarphobe's Guide to Better English in Plain English*. New York: Riverhead Books, 2004.

Sant, Tom. *Persuasive Business Proposals: Writing to Win Customers, Clients, and Contracts*. 2nd ed. New York: AMACOM, 2004.

Strunk, William, and E. B. White. *The Elements of Style*. 4th ed. New York: Longman Publishers, 2000.

INDEX